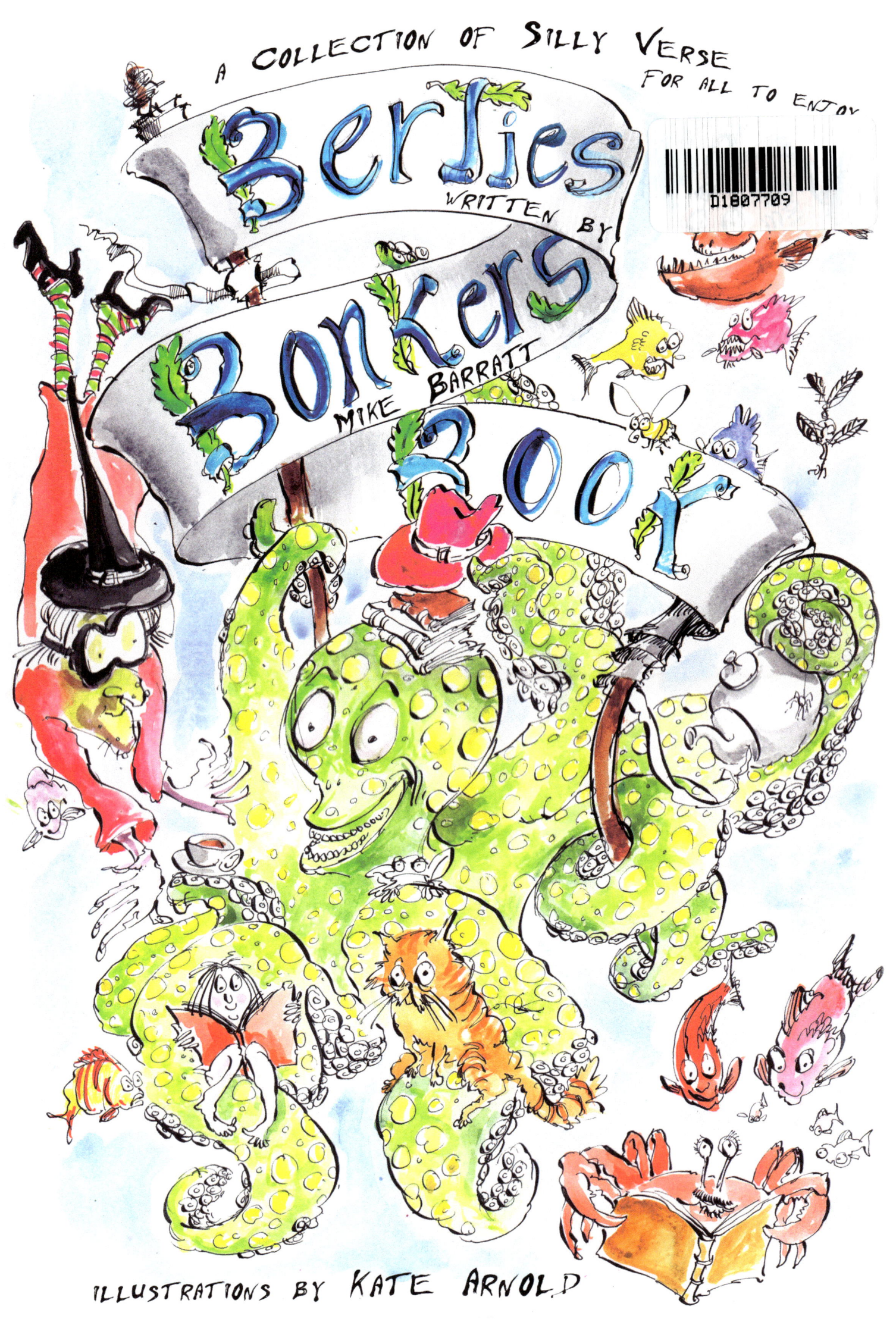

A COLLECTION OF SILLY VERSE
FOR ALL TO ENJOY

Berties Bonkers Book

WRITTEN BY MIKE BARRATT

ILLUSTRATIONS BY KATE ARNOLD

Matador
9 Priory Business Park,
Wistow Road, Kibworth Beauchamp,
Leicestershire. LE8 0RX
Tel: 0116 279 2299
Email: books@troubador.co.uk
Web: www.troubador.co.uk/matador
Twitter: @matadorbooks

ISBN 978 1788037 952

British Library Cataloguing in Publication Data.
A catalogue record for this book is available from the British Library.

Printed and bound by CPI Group (UK) Ltd, Croydon, CR0 4YY

Matador is an imprint of Troubador Publishing Ltd

To Sofia Woolf

There are a few people to thank for getting this book this far: My wife Sue, for believing in me and pushing me to complete it; Mrs Douglas at Carrdus School for words of encouragement which mean a lot from an English teacher; Milli McGregor for her work on design and layout and of course the wonderful Kate Arnold for bringing it all to life with her superb illustrations.

Finally , my two beautiful girls, Megan and Izzy, with whom I have spent very many happy hours reading bedtime stories – I would love to think other parents can do the same with this book!

Sofia — I hope you enjoy this and
it reminds you of your time
at Carrdus!

all the best

Oliver Barratt

Sofia,
Good luck and best wishes
from us all at Carrdus,

Mrs. Way

Contents

QUESTIONS
QUESTIONS

Why do we eat fish fingers, but never fish thumbs

and yet we eat eggs, coming from chicken's bums?

Why is a hot crossed bun in a bad mood

and why do we eat all this funny food?

Why does a snail carry its house on its back

he should settle down, stop, and unpack.

Then he could go faster without all that weight,

but he'd look like a slug and that might not be great.

THE TROUBLE WITH SPACE

There is no gravity in outer space

and stuff just flies all over the place.

You have to be strapped down when lying in bed

to avoid floating off and banging your head.

(So if you're thinking of flying off in a rocket

make sure to put plenty lead in your pocket)

But how can you wee when in outer space

without it hitting you square in the face?

I think you must have to stand on your head

and watch it hit the ceiling instead.

At least I think I would get nice and thin,

Because food would float off, before I stuff it in.

But I don't think that space travel is for me

floating about and dodging my own wee.

It all seems messy and risky and dodgy all round

I think I'll stay put, right here on the ground.

Penguin

I know a penguin who is cuddly and black

and he has feathers all over his back.

He looks like a bit like a duck but he doesn't go quack!

He lives on the ice where it's very cold

and likes to eat fish, or so I'm told.

He doesn't have arms so he can't pick his nose

and he has webbing between all his toes

so he can swim very fast but he can't really run

but he is cute and cuddly and lots of fun.

They live on icebergs and make nests in pairs

and sometimes get eaten by big polar bears.

They wear black suits and they look very posh

like they could be serving some fancy nosh.

I knew one once who trained as a waiter,

but a great big polar bear

came along and ate her.

WHICH?

There once was a witch who lived alone by a ditch.

There was another witch living just down the lane,

She wore the same clothes and she looked just the same.

They both wore black cloaks and a big pointy hat,

and had the obligatory little black cat.

One witch was nice, she was pleasant and kind,

The other was cruel with a horrible mind.

Now, I can't tell you, as I'm not a snitch

So you will have to work out

Which witch is which.

SPINSTER OF THIS PARISH

There is an old lady who lives down our lane,

She's not very tall and she's a little bit vain,

She's never been married and she lives on her own

In her old and decrepit, tumbledown home.

She thinks she is beautiful, gorgeous and fit,

But the truth is exaggerated - just a bit!

She's crooked and ugly with a wart on her nose

and wrinkled hands, and turned up toes.

Her hair is like rats tails and one eye is black

and she's covered in blisters all over her back.

She says men have chased her for many years

especially after too many beers

But she always says "No", she turns them down flat

a nd lives on her own with an old ginger cat.

She says that she always plays hard to get

And after 82 years, she's not been got yet.

 LOOK OUT

If I was a spider I'd spin a big web

and as you passed by I would drop on your head.

You would tremble with fright and cry out in fear

as I burrow my way right inside your ear.

And once I am in there, anything goes

I might even live right there in your nose.

I'd eat all your brain, then have a surprise

at what I could see when I look through your eyes.

But what if you sneezed and I fell to the floor

and got trodden, or squished, or slammed in a door

I could break some legs, or even worse- dead

I think I will eat peanut butter instead.

ABOVE!!

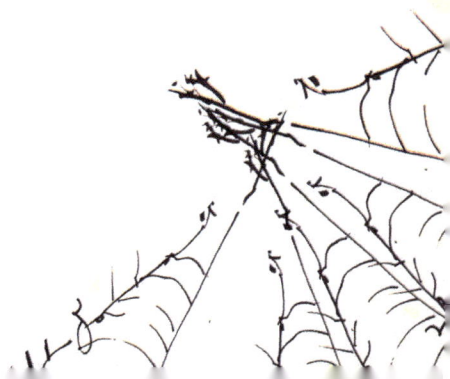

RAPUNZEL

Rapunzel was watching TV in her room

When her stepmother said it's your bedtime soon'

When she wasn't in bed in more than an hour

Her stepmother locked her in a very tall tower.

She fed her on water and bowls of rat stew

And over the years her hair grew and grew.

A Prince heard of her plight and decided to phone

But her voicemail said "the Princess isn't home".

He got in his car and did 90 miles an hour

And soon he was standing at the base of the tower.

'Rapunzel' he shouted when he got there

"Please let me try to climb up your hair"

So arm over arm, he started to climb,

and was soon halfway up in record time

But soon he was in trouble.

And that trouble was big...

To his horror he discovered she was wearing a wig!

It was such a tragic fall from grace

As the Prince fell flat, on his regal face.

SLEEPING BEAUTY

The Princess was bored of reading her kindle

So she found an old loom with a very sharp spindle

She decided to spin a nice shawl she could keep

But she pricked her finger, and fell fast asleep.

She instantly fell into a very deep slumber

And lay there as still as a big fat cucumber.

Years went by and she laid on her bed

and a thick layer of dust formed on her head

her toenails grew as long as cats claws

and her fingernails grew right down to the floor.

Hair grew in her nose, and wax filled her ears

And she started to stink as she lay there for years.

As news of this spread all over the land

An ugly prince took matters in hand

He thought this is too good to miss

And rushed in the room to give her a kiss

The Princess awoke, and sat bolt upright,

And said "Gosh you are ugly, you gave me a fright;

I was having a lovely peaceful 4,000 winks

Now get out of here, your breath really stinks.

Listen to Your Parents

Izzy was fed up she said with a sigh

"I can't stand it I wonder why

I have to listen each and every day

to the stupid rules my parents say

If you don't eat your crusts you will have curly hair

If you step on a crack you will marry a bear

They are stupid sayings and never right

Why, without carrots I can still see at night!

If you don't brush regularly your teeth will fall out

That's just a big lie - what's that all about?

If you pick your nose you don't get a disease

There's just less to come out when you have to sneeze".

So she ignored all the advice, she just didn't care

And when she grew up she married a bear

Her hair was dull and awfully straight

And at nightime her eyesight wasn't that great

Her teeth all fell out and she looked quite a sight

Too late she realised her parents were right.

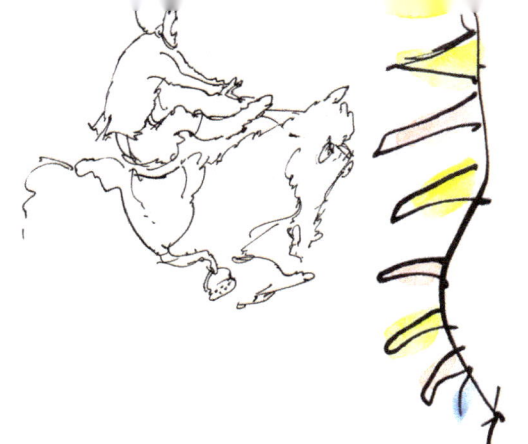

UNICORN

At the stables one day, a new notice went up

Entries now open for the Oakfield House Cup.

Megan read the big sign and sighed - 'oh if only

- but I don't even have my very own pony'.

Dad took her to the pet shop to see what was in stock,

but when they got there, they were in for a shock.

"We sell goldfish and rabbits and puppy dogs only

Its really quite silly to think we'd have a

pony".

Megan's face was a picture all sad and

forlorn

Then the owner said 'wait -

how about a Unicorn"

'That'll do 'said Dad,

"Ill take it of course,

cos he knew it was just a new breed of horse.

'Oh great' thought Megan - "I'll" never be able

To beat stuck up Finella from Wobbly Hall Stable

She has the best horse, the best saddle and bridle

And has always been my number one rival.

So she put the unicorn into intensive training

And even rode him when it was raining.

He learnt all the moves and was swift, slick and steady

And after three months they thought he was ready.

The big day came the Oakfield House Cup

Finella was first, and she soon saddled up.

She was good, smooth and slick

Her pony just flowed without using the stick,

Her 10 metre circle was perfect and round

And she seemed to be floating just off the ground.

Then it was Megan, so she went into the ring

The crowd laughed but she didn't notice a

thing.

She circled and trotted and cantered in

time

And came to a halt on the centre line.

She smiled at the judge who gave her a clap

And she hopped down excitedly from Unicorn's back.

The judge debated with a frown on his face

And declared - 'There is a tie for first place.

It's between Megan and Finella from Wobbly Hall

The scores are tied there's no difference at all.

But in the tiebreak - it's the Unicorn

Who gets 5 extra points for sounding his horn"

GARDENING

I planted some sheep dogs deep in the ground

and covered them over and trampled around.

I watered them daily and waited to see

if they would grow as big a tree.

I sat and watched for many an hour

but I didn't even get one Collie Flower.

So I bought some bird seed and scattered it around

evenly spread all over the ground

but that was a bitter disappointment too

out of the whole packet

- not one single bird grew.

Cauliflower

THE FUSSY FISH

There once was a fish who lived in the sea

who was as fussy as any fussy fish could be.

If she could have just one granted wish

she would change the toilet habits of fish.

Her first words every morning would always be

"Mummy, where can I go to have a wee?"

Her mum would answer her too fussy daughter

"my darling, just here, in this patch of water",

Every morning she'd shreak - "urgh - I cant do it here,

to wee in the water - that's dirty and queer"

"I cant do it here, why what will they think

when my friends all want a   nice cooling drink?

Can you imagine the   shock and horrid surprise

Of getting warm wee   straight in your eyes?

I really don't think that   a nice girl fish oughta

Do it right here in the   clean drinking water"

But I have decided, I   know what I'm to do.

I will swim away and find   a nice loo.

So she swam round the seas,   the river and lake,

She asked every Cod every Haddock and Hake

But not one of them pointed a solitary fin

at a nice flushing toilet a girl could go in.

By now she was desperate, getting red in the face

as she darted and swam all over the place

"I cant do it here, I would rather die first

and that's what she did, she swelled up and burst.

Her mother wasn't sad that her daughter was dead

"Theres plenty more fish in the sea", she said.

IF HOW AND WHY?

If a Cat were a Dog would it still chase a Cat?

If a Bat married Cricket would they have cricket bats?

If a Bee got squashed would it be B flat?

I think it would be dead, or something like that.

And here's one that's a bit of a riddle

Why is Piggy always in the middle?

Why is a Toad in the hole

but never a Frog,

And how can a sausage

be called a hot dog?

If you put a leek in a bowl,

would it all seep out?

And what is raining Cats and Dogs all about?

Does a Stick insect

have a family tree?

These are all questions

that are puzzling me. **?**

THE BEE AND THE WASP

A young bee was sitting on a flower one day

when a bright coloured wasp flew her way.

"Oh, he's so handsome" was all she could say

and she couldn't stop talking about him all day

"He's the most handsome bee I've ever seen,

so bright, so colourful, fit and lean.

He's not fat like other boy bees,

I think I would like to marry him, please.

So her friends set out to find the young bee

to see what all the fuss could be.

They thought they'd found him -

but it was his brother

(after all one wasp looks much like another).

At last they found the young chap

and the all gathered round and started to clap

"Oh you're such a handsome bee" they said

The young wasp just smiled and

scratched his head.

"Our friend wants to marry you straight away"

The wasp just shrugged and said 'ok'

"Is he really a wasp?"

Some friends whispered, a little concerned

Wasps and bees didn't marry,

or so they had learned.

But the wedding was set for the very next day

and all the preparations were well under way.

Now according to bee law a veil must be worn,

And not lifted until all the vows have been sworn.

So the young bee wore a veil

that was worn by her mother

and a great, great aunt or someone or other.

And on the next day she walked down the aisle

her face was covered, but full of a smile.

The vicar droned on they all sang a song

Bee weddings are boring and take very long

There's lots of singing and chanting and things

And clever coordinated flapping of wings.

There's a collection pot to be

filled up with honey

(because of course bees don't have real money).

The congregation was buzzing

as at last the vicar said

"The wedding is over, I declare you wed

Yes!" cried the bee lifting her veil

But then she discovered the sting in the tail.

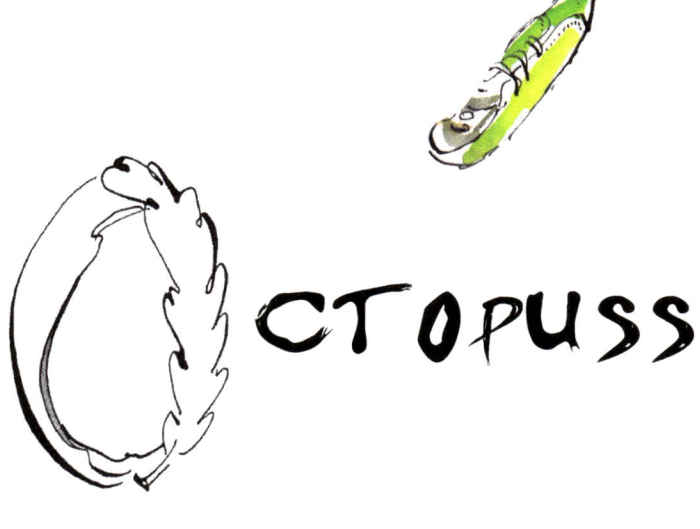
CTOPUSS

There once was an octopus who had to go shopping,

his shoes were too tight and he'd starting hopping,

"They're killing my feet" he would moan and complain

so he left for the city on the very next train.

He found a shop that was brimming with shoes

in so many colours it was so hard to choose.

He tried them all on, every last single pair

but didn't really find what we wanted in there.

The next shop was bigger, it went on for miles

with lace ups, and boots, in all sorts of styles.

After hours of trying he found some slip ons

Bright yellow and green - yes! these were the ones

But sadly he left with tears in his eyes

The shop only had three pairs in his size.

My Sister
Put the Cat in the Washer

My sister put the cat in the washer

Which gave it a terrible fright

She put it on non fast coloureds

And shut the door for the night.

My sister put the cat in the washer

It created a terrible din

It didn't like Daz or Ariel

And it hated super fast spin.

My sister put the cat in the washer

She said it smelt like a skunk

But after a 40 degree cycle

The poor thing had actually shrunk.

My sister put the cat in the washer

Now it's only got eight lives to go

It came out smelling of springtime

From it's head to the tip of it's toe.

My Sister put the cat in the washer

She must have been out of her head

The poor things allergic to water

I think we'll get her

a goldfish instead.

THE INSECTS CUP FINAL

The insects cup final was one fine summers day

The millipede was desperately hoping to play

But when the teams were announced he was only a sub

so he went to his room and started to blub.

One the day of the match he sat on the line

and peeled all the oranges for his teams half time.

The match was quite tight, it was real nip and tuck

as they rolled round and got filthy, in all kinds of muck.

The spiders scuttled and the ladybirds flew

and quite where the ball was, nobody knew.

The ball went up front and the slug tried and tried

but half an hour later he was still caught offside.

Then a bird ate a fly that was in the home team...

Millipede was going to play! it's just like his dream.

But by the time he'd got 50 pairs of boots on

the match was all over and everyone gone.